The Let's Talk Library™

Let's Talk About Feeling Lonely

Melanie Ann Apel

The Rosen Publishing Group's
PowerKids Press™
New York

To my "pen pal" Wade Brown, with whom I began writing many years ago. Love, Melanie

Published in 2001 by The Rosen Publishing Group, Inc.
29 East 21st Street, New York, NY 10010

First Edition

Book Design: Maria Melendez

Photo Credits: pp. 8, 11, 19 © FPG International; pp. 4, 7 © Index Stock; pp. 12, 15, 16, 20 © International Stock.

Apel, Melanie Ann.
    Let's talk about feeling lonely / by Melanie Ann Apel.
        p. cm.— (Let's talk about library)
    Includes index.
    Summary: Defines loneliness, discusses different situations that can cause it, and suggests ways of dealing with it.
    ISBN 0-8239-5620-2 (alk. paper)
    1. Loneliness in children—Juvenile literature. [1. Loneliness.] I. Title. II. Series.
    BF723.L64 A64 2000
    152.4—dc21   00-023838

Manufactured in the United States of America.

Table of Contents

Amanda

Amanda's dad just left for work. Her brother Jake is at school. Her mom is with her baby sister Lauren. Amanda asks her mom, "Will you take me to the playground?"

Her mom says, "I can't take you to the playground now, Amanda. I'm busy with the baby."

"Can you play a game with me then?" Amanda asks.

"Later honey," her mom tells her. "I really have to take care of your sister now."

"Then who should I play with?" Amanda asks. Amanda is feeling very lonely.

◀ *When there is no one around to play with, you might feel lonely.*

What Is Loneliness?

Loneliness is an **emotion** or feeling. It is the sadness you feel when you are alone. You might feel sad because there might not be people around to do things with you. Maybe there are people around, but no one you know well. This can make you feel lonely, too. Are there times when you have felt lonely? Did your loneliness go away? It feels bad to be lonely, but the painful feelings will get better with time.

Doing something new, like starting at a different school, can make you feel lonely. ▶

Who Gets Lonely?

Everyone feels lonely once in a while. People who work at home instead of in an office might feel lonely sometimes. People who live in the country and don't have neighbors can get lonely, too. **Elderly** people who live in **nursing homes** get lonely. They miss their families. People who travel alone might miss seeing familiar faces. When you get lonely, remember that it is a feeling everybody deals with from time to time.

◀ *People in nursing homes miss their families. This woman is happy to be spending time with her granddaughter.*

Loneliness Hurts

When you feel lonely, you might feel nervous or **anxious**. Maybe you worry that you will always feel lonely. Your body might hurt, too. You might feel empty inside. Loneliness can actually make your heart seem like it is very heavy. These feelings are uncomfortable, but they also remind you to pay attention to your emotions. Never forget that your feelings are important. If you take your feelings seriously, so will other people. Then you will feel better about asking for help if you need it.

Always pay attention to how you are feeling. When you take your feelings seriously, other people will, too. ▶

Rob's Tree House

Rob likes to climb up to his tree house. He brings along his favorite book, a bottle of juice, and a small bag of red licorice. Rob loves his family, but sometimes he likes to be alone. His older sister might be watching a television show he doesn't like. Maybe his baby brother is fussing and making a lot of noise. In his tree house, Rob can have quiet time to read, draw, or just daydream.

◄ *These kids are having fun playing together. It is also important to have time alone to do the things you like most.*

Alone but Not Lonely

People can spend time alone without feeling lonely. Sometimes people enjoy having the time and space to do just what they like. When people have busy lives, it is important to take a break to be alone. When they feel rested, they will have energy for all the things they need to do. They will enjoy the other people in their lives more. Needing time alone has nothing to do with how much you love your friends or family. We all need to be by ourselves once in a while.

This boy likes having time by himself to work on his drawing. ▶

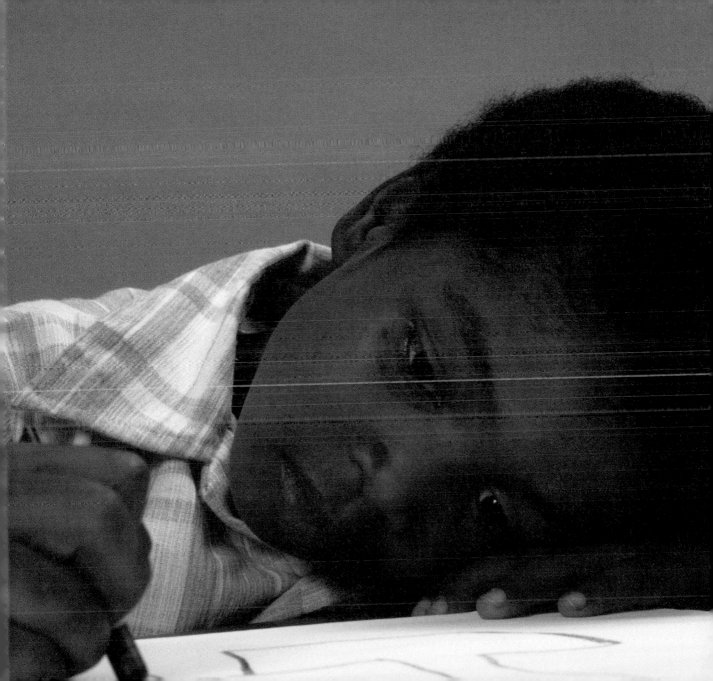

Brittany

Brittany lives in a **foster home** with three other kids. In a foster home, adults take care of children who are not their relatives. There is always something going on at Brittany's house. Her foster mom and dad are busy taking care of Brittany's foster brothers and sisters, especially the one-year-old twins. Brittany shares a room with her older foster sister Heather. Sometimes Heather does not pay attention to Brittany. Heather will also talk about things that do not interest Brittany. Even with all these people around, Brittany sometimes feels lonely.

◀ *Sharing a room can be a lot of fun. There will be times when the other person is busy, though. Then you might feel lonely.*

Feeling Lonely With Others Around

Sometimes you may feel lonely even when you are with a lot of people. Maybe you and your family have just moved. When you go to your new school on the first day, you will not know anyone. This could make you feel lonely. You might have problems, but no special friend to talk to about them. This can make you feel lonely, too. In time you will make friends, even a special best friend with whom you can share your secrets. At first though, facing something new can make you feel very lonely.

When you first move to a different town, you might feel lonely. Be patient, though. You will make friends. ▶

How to Feel Less Lonely

You can do things to help yourself feel less lonely. If there is no one around to play with, read a book. Enjoy the story and the adventures of the **characters** in the book. Call a friend. Clean your room. Write a letter or an e-mail to someone. Write in your journal or diary. Sometimes writing down how you feel can make you feel better. You could even write a story and have the main characters figure out ways to feel less lonely. Getting **involved** in an activity you enjoy is another great way to get rid of those lonely feelings.

◀ *This boy loves to spend time reading. He does not feel lonely, even though he is by himself.*

Helping Yourself by Helping Someone Else

A great way to feel less lonely is to get involved in helping someone else. One of your friends might be feeling lonely. Try talking to him. You might not make all of his bad feelings go away, but knowing you care will mean a lot to him. **Focusing** on someone else will also make you feel better. You'll see that loneliness is an emotion we all share. You'll feel good about yourself for taking the time to help out your friend.

Glossary

anxious (AYNK-shus) Uneasy or worried.

characters (KAYR-ik-turz) People in a story.

elderly (EL-der-lee) People who are older than middle age.

emotion (ih-MOH-shun) A strong feeling, such as anger or sadness.

focusing (FOH-cus-ing) Concentrating.

foster home (FOS-tur HOHM) A home where children live when they cannot live with their families.

involved (in-VOLVD) To be kept busy by something.

nursing homes (NER-sing HOMZ) Places for people who need special, long-term medical care.

23

Index